Manners in School

Arianna Candell · Rosa M. Curto

BOOK HOUSE

Back to school

John is going to a new school, but he doesn't want to go. He doesn't know his teacher or anyone in his class and he doesn't even know where to find his classroom. Anna sees that John is very sad. She takes his hand and leads him into school. John is in the same class as Anna and they soon become good friends.

Paul

Anna

John

Wake up early

Anna wakes up early. She is always first to arrive at school but Peter is often late. Snuggled under his blankets, he never wants to get up. Then he remembers that all his classmates will be waiting for him in class, so he jumps up quickly!
Do you wake up early?

Anna

John

Maria

Peter

Rosie

Archie

learn to be patient

Today the children are learning to make things out of clay. Peter is really good at making animals! Lily is not as patient as Peter. She is upset because she just can't seem to make the shapes properly. Peter is kind and he helps her. Now she likes working with clay and is making an animal, too.

Peter

Lily

Washing your hands

The children have so much fun in the playground! They play ball, skip, or dig in the sandpit. When they go back into the classroom, all the kids have to wash their hands. Anna doesn't want to wait her turn at the sink and goes straight to her seat at the table. Lily tells her that she'll make their school books dirty if she doesn't wash her hands.

Rachel

Anna

Lily

Mo

Rosie

Adrian

David

Jake

Alex

John

Maria

John

Rachel

Learning to share

The books and toys in school are for everyone to share. Rosie's big brother always lets her borrow his box of coloured pencils. But when Rosie brings her new storybook to school, she doesn't want anyone to borrow it. The she realises that the other kids like reading new stories just as much as she does. So she decides to share her book with them.

Rosie

Everybody, play!

Games in the playground or classroom are better fun when more children join in! Mo and Lucy love playing football, and they ask the other kids to come and play with them. They both know that it's more fun when you include everyone. So all the schoolchildren get a chance to play.

Adrian

Mo

Rosie

Lucy

Is everybody ready?

Lily

David

Mo

Maria

Today the children are going to paint a picture to take home. But they can't begin because Maria is still walking around. Everyone must be sitting down and ready before they can start. Mo asks her to sit next to him so they can start painting. At last, Maria sees that everyone is waiting and she rushes back to her seat!

John

Rachel

Quiet!

School started a few days ago and John is feeling much happier in his new class. He has so many friends and so much to talk about! He even talks when he should be working quietly or listening to his teacher. Some of the children can't hear what their teacher is saying so they ask John to be quiet. He must learn when to talk and when to pay attention.

Anna

Lily

David

Archie

That's not funny

David and Rachel like to mess around in class and tease their classmates! Their jokes aren't always funny. Sometimes their jokes are cruel, and nobody else laughs. Jokes are only funny when everyone can enjoy them.

Rachel

Pick up and clean up

After playing and working, it's time to clear up. All the toys must be put away. The wastepaper scraps need to be picked up. The paint brushes need washing and all the scissors and pencils need to go back on the shelf. Everyone knows this, but they don't always do it. John's class had a good idea. Every day, it's someone's job to make sure that everybody helps to keep the classroom clean. Today, it's Adrian's turn.

Lucy

Rachel

Lily

Adrian

Paul

Rosie

Archie

Rosie

Helping each other

How high can you count? Did you know that you can never finish counting? Numbers are infinite – that means that they go on forever. Archie and Rosie love counting. Lucy and David find counting really hard. They are all friends so they help each other. This makes the work easier for Lucy and David to understand. So now they all enjoy their work more!

Lucy

David

Let's talk about it

Peter knows that hitting other kids doesn't mean you're stronger or braver. He tells Lily that some kids just haven't learned to solve their problems by talking about them. He knows that words can help you to make friends. Instead of having fights, try to find the answer to your problem by talking about it, like Peter does.

Mo

you're lucky!

It's the end of the first week. The children are all learning to work together as a class. They have learned to respect and help each another, and this is just as important as all their school lessons. They are very lucky because they have already learned to share so much together.

Mo

Archie

David

Lucy

Rosie

Rosie

Archie

Lucy

Everyone is
different

Anna

David

Mo

Peter

Adrian

Lily

Maria

As you have seen, not everyone is good at the same things. We can help each another by sharing what we are good at. Everyone is different, and we can always learn something new from another person.

John

Rachel

Activities

Maria

LISTENING FOR SILENCE

You must be absolutely quiet for this activity. No-one can make any kind of noise. Everyone must sit quietly for one minute and listen. During this silence, you will hear noises. Someone may move a chair, a car outside may toot its horn, or thunder may boom in the sky. You will discover that during this minute's silence, not everyone will have heard the same noises. Remember to listen very carefully. Now find out what noises everyone heard.

CLASSROOM GAMES

When we have finished our work, the teacher sometimes lets us play. We love to play a game of finding something that has been hidden. Someone is chosen to hide a small object in the classroom while the rest of us cover our eyes.The object must be hidden but still possible to see. We then try to spot it without leaving our seats. The game is to find the object by searching only with our eyes! Whoever finds it gets to hide the next object.

We like another game that tests our memory! Eight or ten small objects are chosen and placed on a table. Everyone looks at them for a short time. Then they are covered with a piece of cloth.

Players take turns naming one of the objects under the cloth. The game is over if no-one can remember what was there, or when everything has been guessed.

Lucy

Lily

Archie

Mo

THE OBSTACLE COURSE

Do you remember that we talked about all the kids playing together? The more players, the more fun it is. Are you ready to start having fun with your classmates?

A teacher can help you prepare an obstacle race in the playground. In this kind of race, you don't run in a straight line. Instead, you have to run around obstacles you find in the way. You can use anything as an obstacle: upturned wastepaper bins or boxes, stools or paintpots. Space them far enough apart so you have room to zigzag around them. When you get to the end, turn and come back again, now jumping over each obstacle until you reach the beginning again...

Which way was the fastest – zig-zagging or jumping?

Anna

CHECKING THE REGISTER

Everyday the teacher has to call out the names on the register to check that everyone is present. Why not try this new, helpful way to check who's in class each day?

Cut out one small piece of cardboard for each pupil in the class. Then ask everyone to write their name on both sides of the card, using a green pencil on one side and a red pencil on the other side.

The teacher can help you sort out the cards so you can pin them onto the classroom noticeboard in alphabetical order. Every day, it can be a different boy or girl's job to read out the names. If everyone is present, the names on the cards will all be green, but if someone is missing, their card will be turned to the red side. This is a good way to help your teacher check attendance, isn't it?

David

 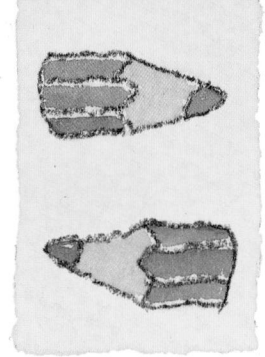   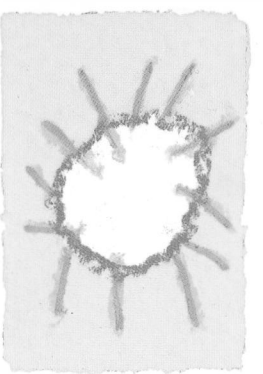 

Guidelines for parents

GOING TO SCHOOL

The first part of this book may help your child to understand that going to school can be difficult at first. Explain that going to school will help them to get ready for adult life. Talk about all the exciting activities that they will do in the classroom. Emphasise that they will meet lots of new friends there. Some early classroom friendships may last a lifetime.

Also explain that being able to go to school is actually a privilege because some children don't get the opportunity to go to school. In many countries, children must work or take care of younger brothers and sisters. They don't have the chance to learn how to read, write, draw or have fun doing other school activities.

LET'S TALK ABOUT IT!

We know that children do have fights. It's still up to us as parents to discourage aggression by teaching our children how to solve problems by talking them through. Explain that not everyone will want to be their friend but they can still talk to them to try to solve their differences. We should also explain how important it is to admit that we have made a mistake. Learning to apologise is the most important lesson in repairing relationships.

   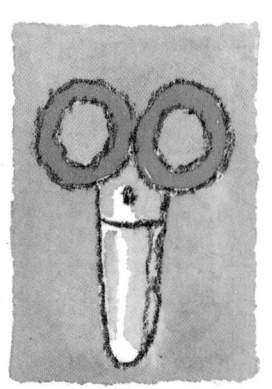 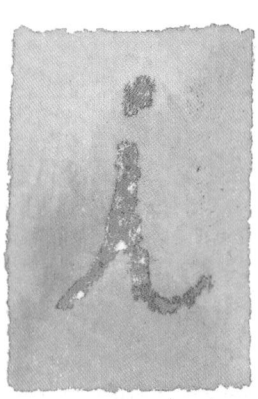 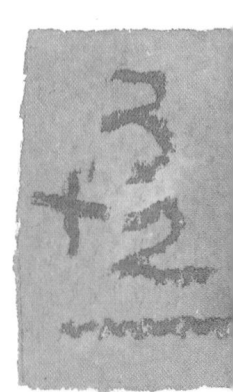

  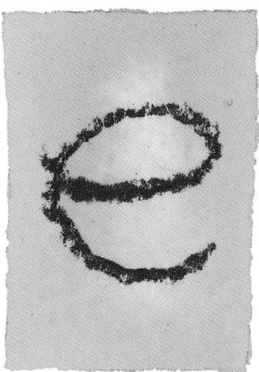   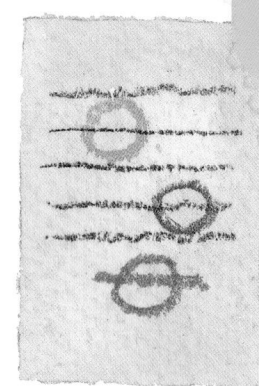

HELP!

We saw that Lily had difficulty making clay figures. Peter was quick to help her. This positive attitude should be emphasised as you read the story aloud. It is very satisfying to see children co-operating and helping one another. It should also be stressed that no-one does everything perfectly or is good at every activity. We must encourage our children to help others and also to ask for help themselves when they need it. There is always someone willing to lend a hand.

GETTING THINGS DONE

We discussed the importance of getting up in time to get ready for school. Children should be reminded not to be late. It's very important to get to places on time so that you don't keep others waiting. Being punctual will be important throughout life. Parents must be on time for work and children must be on time for school. Even very young children should understand that they have duties and responsibilities.

CLEAN AND TIDY

Many children do not like to tidy up, or think it's not important to have clean hands. Ask these children if they would like to live in a very messy, untidy house. Ask them if they would mind if their parents prepared meals with dirty hands. Parents should provide strong role models for their children to copy so they don't pick up bad habits from their friends.

Children should be taught early on that it's important that they help keep their classrooms and play areas neat and tidy. If everyone pitches in and helps put things away, tidying up is much faster. And it will benefit everyone because if the toys and supplies are always put back where they belong, they can easily be found again.

Parents should encourage this spirit of co-operation and the need to be tidy at home. Young children enjoy taking part in family chores and helping mum and dad. In the process, they develop a feeling of self-worth which they can carry with them into adulthood.

    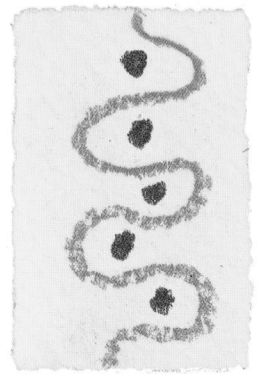 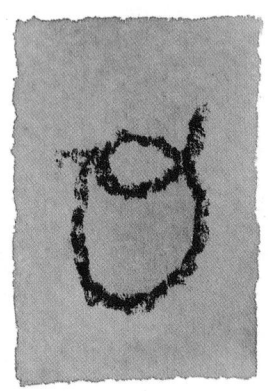

Published in Great Britain in MMXII by
Book House, an imprint of
The Salariya Book Company Ltd
25 Marlborough Place, Brighton BN1 1UB
www.salariya.com
www.book-house.co.uk

1 3 5 7 9 8 6 4 2

A CIP catalogue record for this book is available
from the British Library.

Printed and bound in China.

PB ISBN: 978-1-908177-12-4

Original title of the book in Catalan: Com ens hem de comportar a l'escola
© MMV Gemser Publications S.L.